Lookinglasshouse

poems by

Al Russell

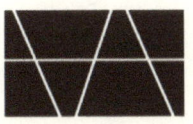

Cover art by Sheena Eastman

Lookinglasshouse **©2021** by **Al Russell**. Published in the United States by Vegetarian Alcoholic Poetry. Not one part of this work may be reproduced without expressed written consent from the author. For more information, please write V.A. Poetry, 643 South 2nd Street, Milwaukee, WI 54204

Lookinglasshouse

9 Learning
10 Talismans
12 Nature's Tenderizer
13 For Clarity's Sake
15 *Amarcord*
16 Rocking Chair
17 When I Was a Kid I Wanted to Be a Boy
18 Naomi with the Long Black Hair
19 Evening Star V
20 Monument to Airmen
21 Poem for Lena Horne
22 Wide Spaces
23 Rimbaud's Emeralds
24 Kid
25 Adolescent
26 Crater Face
27 Mark
28 Year of the Bird Man
29 Letter to a Dead Man
30 April: For a Friend Whom I Consider Dead
31 Date Night
32 Stuttering Aubade
33 Marry Me
34 No Exit
35 A Girl in (Jackson) Library
36 Evening on Karl Johan Street
37 Summer
38 Cicada
39 Shelter from the Storm
40 Killing Light
42 Vacuum
43 *Audition*
45 Fire Woman/Ice Man
46 Between Two Rivers
47 Cohesion at 3:00
48 1949
49 Organ Harvest: Laconia
50 Every Photograph of You is a Photograph of When You Were Younger
51 The Thing About Shapes in Lookinglasshouse
52 I Didn't Believe the Stories

53 "Getting old ain't the end of the world. Dying is."
54 Space Baby
55 Space Dogs
56 Pine Inlet
57 Hanging Rock Lake
58 Bridge Overlooking the Seine
59 Disturbing Portrait of my Father, Sketched by My Grandmother
60 Janus
61 Parish Priest
62 Ars Poetica
63 Fragments of Buson
64 Wedding Poem
65 Domesticity
66 Revelations
67 Parish Priest Redux
68 America
69 Over the Border
71 Love Lies Sleeping II
72 Awake
73 100 BPM
74 Every Time I Hear You Cough I Think You're Dying
75 Halo
76 Heaven and Earth
77 After Man
78 Like Frida Kahlo's Burning Bed

Acknowledgments

I Didn't Believe the Stories and *Crater Face* were in *Squawk Back* May 2020

For Clarity's Sake and *Hanging Rock Lake* were in *The Fabulist Words and Art* August 2020

Like Frida Kahlo's Burning Bed was in *Nonbinary Review* #23

This book is dedicated to all y'all who raised me, but especially my Mom.

Everything in this autobiographical journey is totally real and completely happened in real life. All of it. Especially the aliens.

"They that hate me without cause are more than the hairs of mine head: they that would destroy me, being mine enemies wrongfully, are mighty: then I restored that which I took not away.

O God, thou knowest my foolishness; and my sins are not hid from thee.

Let not them that wait on thee, O Lord God of hosts, be ashamed for my sake: let not those that seek thee be confounded for my sake, O God of Israel.

Because for thy sake I have borne reproach: shame hath covered my face.

I am become a stranger unto my brethren, and an alien unto my mother's children.

For the zeal of thine house hath eaten me up; and the reproaches of them that reproached thee are fallen upon me.

When I wept, and chastened my soul with fasting, that was to my reproach.

I made sackcloth also my garment; and I became a proverb to them.

They that sit at the gate speak against me; and I was the song of the drunkards.

But as for me, my prayer is unto thee, O Lord, in an acceptable time: O God, in the multitude of thy mercy hear me, in the truth of thy salvation.

Deliver me out of the mire, and let me not sink: let me be delivered from them that hate me, and out of the deep waters.

Let not the water-flood overthrow me, neither let the deep swallow me up, and let not the pit shut her mouth upon me.

Hear me, O Lord, for thy loving kindness is good: turn unto me according to the multitude of thy tender mercies.

And hide not thy face from thy tender servant; for I am in trouble: hear me speedily.

Draw nigh unto my soul, and redeem it: deliver me because of mine enemies.

Thou hast known my reproach, and my shame, and my dishonor: mine adversaries are all before thee.

Reproach hath broken my heart; and I am full of heaviness: and I looked for some to take the pity, but there was none; and for comforters, but I found none."

PSALM 69, VERSE 4-20

Learning

Child has a face.
Child has a face smeared with beans.
Child has a face smeared with beans
and apple sauce.
Child knows from its mother what lips do.
Child draws weather patterns
in blue marker
on white linen table cloth.
Child makes paper airplane
destroy paper airplane.
Looks to the sky:
MARRY ME LIZ
written in bold marshmallow letters.
Answers.

Talismans

We three do the Steve Martin, hieroglyphic palms
flat outstretched each to receive the others,

our weird mating dance for the cops
in the next lane, daring them with our eyes

as we go by. You fidget with the Monopoly piece,
the dog, on the dashboard. It is as good as a Saint

Christopher and just as holy, you bought the defunct
board game at a flea market. We cross a bridge

over the Yadkin River and blue lights, you bet
your girl in the seat beside you five bucks

the sirens are not for us. The gold alligator
hanging from the rearview protests. We threw

the smoke out the window five miles
back, the lights wouldn't be

for that. The car is registered to us and we
haven't seriously littered all day. Fingernails

of the girl's tick nervously at her jewelry, a rosary
of dried olive pits. The cop could be a fan

of smooth cooing into wadded cotton type crooning
or shrill crunchy fuzzy-bassed arena rock

but too homophobic for drum machines, synth,
eyeliner, precise mathematics of the New Wave.

What if he saw the holy books of the Church
of the Subgenius gunking up the rear window?

Either way the sirens are encroaching.
We're nearing the county line. An incredulous look

on your face. *Calm down,* you say to everyone
in the Caddy: me, and your girl, and mostly
yourself: *They can't arrest us for dancing.*

Nature's Tenderizer

So many bodies
were dredged up from the bottom
of the swash, in a crab trap,
it had been weeks
and their skins were falling off
in flaky green chunks
like cheese sliced in blocks
with an improper knife.
There was no room for crabs in the wire box
but some of the bodies
whose clothes had rotted off
still wore gold jewelry:
the last dignity of the eaten.
And they *were* eaten—
what the fish and sea scum didn't finish
we roasted and gorged on, happy the meat
had first gone through nature's tenderizer.

For Clarity's Sake

In my house a grubby shower stall
is where I bathe myself. It smells
deep, populated mostly
by pipe sucking harvestmen.

I'd like a big claw
-footed bathtub like
the one I
used to have,
so I could sculpt,
like a soufflé, a bubble
bath relief map
with a chasm
of a Nordic fjord to represent
the warring factions
of the Bubble People
who all look foamy, juicy blue and light
but have decided
they are different and don't
get along.

In a more inventive
child's mind they might be
overhead projector transparencies,
insides scribbled
in squeaky red grease pen,
squirt bottles of blue glass cleaner,
Cinderella's shoes and surprised face.

And how
do these wars support
their (allegedly)
nontoxic
ways
of
life?
I have to let them
destroy one another
my own interference would be too much

they'd blow all away
with a puff of my breath
on a strain of glassy air.

Amarcord

Three years old: Chicken Hair.
Blonde wisps blown straight up by wind.

Clara, mother of us all
laughing that laugh
—dry cough in waves—
the ocean breeze.

End of the day
we've caught nothing
Pabst Blue Ribbon,
Bud Light cans
uncle's piss off the side of the boat.

Chicken Hair licks the green paint
the name, *Whoa Nellie*, in metallic sparkles.
Does it taste of the color
it shares with the ocean?

"Hey, you"
. . . through the transistor's
crack and hum . . .
Then:
"Come here! Come here!"

Clara's gray eyebrows dance,
tongue rolls,
grabs the tiny hand
in her bony claw.
"One day,"
she croaks,
"you'll be as old as me."
Then:

POOF she is gone
and I am left
in my thirties
standing naked
in a humid parking lot.

Rocking Chair

Rocking Chair
Porch Swing
Rope Tire
Teeter Totter
over
the edge of a whirl-
pool—
I am going to fall!
BACKWARD!
I am going to get eaten
by this Barcalounger
this Sofa Bed
this big metal-springed mouth with its red
velvet tongue
I will get motion-
sick and crazy-scared,
I and the cat will get trapped in
there and hurtle into oblivion

When I Was a Kid I Wanted to Be a Boy

I was playing Peter Pan
in my father's old fedora
with the feather in the brim.
I dressed my infant brother
in a doll's blue nightgown.
The cat and the koala
and the friendly yellow gator
made the front row of the choir
of Lost Boys who got the sermon.

My nine-year-old cousin stormed in,
he yelled about the dress
I'd stuffed my brother into:
"Don't you see?! You can't do that to people!
You can't do that!"

Naomi with the Long Black Hair

Your mother made
you wear a trash bag
to school because
you couldn't afford
a pretty bright
yellow or lavender
rain slicker
like the other kids'.
Lookit,
they're pastels
in the down-
pour but don't
smudge or bleed

(or bleed or bleed).

You are just a mincing
gnat and teacher
catches you like
she's an exotic
carnivorous plant
with false eye-
lashes for teeth
and tells you to
go sit with
the others and they
look at you
like you stink
and don't say
anything.

What is it
like to have
a happy heart
and not hide behind
the large front
door columns
pretending to be
one of the boxed
lunches?

Evening Star V

Hill with no grass
pink puffy hand-me-down parka
frost-spun dirt
cockatiel preening my father's black beard.
Watercolors from under my wet nails crying down newsprint.
Sighing and learning. Void of no void.
Hear things as I see them,
foggy, misshapen,
obstructed by my light head.
Put on my listening
ears to read and everyone sounds
like braying geese.

From the Painting by Georgia O'Keeffe

Monument to Airmen

I
Only Gladys, goddess
of our side, of askew
goggles and nylon underwear,
tobacco pipes, manna, and washing soap,
can save you now.
She is a gorgeous
lavender shadowed
with pink,
razored with blue.
She is still clouds at night.

II
It is 1993. What are you doing
with your life?

"I'm only six."

Get it together, Small Idiot,
in the Big Leagues you don't have to ask
when to go to the bathroom.

III
after this candle toppled to the floor

IV
The human spirit is Perseverance.
They told us that in school.
I hope they're right, I hope we all get such
a beautiful angel
as the Tuskegee Airmen did.

From the Sculpture by Selma Burke

Poem for Lena Horne

Her voice echoes
through a corridor
of trees, blows the ragged
branches, verdigris almost
tumbleweeding along parched,
scorched earth.
Don't shoot that dog
outside that clapboard shack,
don't shoot that man
standing in the middle of a field
staring at the sky with grey,
filmed-over eyes.
I hope it will rain.

Wide Spaces

They are what Lou
at fifteen dreams of,
not the porthole windows
of his bricked-in basement room,
the floor of cold cement
masked by black vinyl,
the frosted glass to outside
six feet from it,
a foot by a foot,
barely seen through on tiptoes.
Lou writes funny limericks
to show to girls with bouncy breasts
in gym class when they're musky with sweet sweat,
takes nips from his parents' piney gin bottles, makes shriveled pruney faces,
spins Duke Ellington's "Solitude" over and over. Lou thinks each plunked note sounds
like a blue-green bubble
bursting inside a diamond.

Rimbaud's Emeralds

This weird city
with its anthropomorphic walls
bleeding cuts like snakes.

This cut on my finger
makes my skin
smell loudly, raw pork.

This talking head saying
"I don't care, I'm blind."
This light and shadow,
this silence.

Kid

I remember her, bright
orange quarter
covering her big teeth,

citrus spark winking
her premature
crow's feet.

Carnies painted
a pastel balloon bunch
on her left cheek,

echo: purple Sharpie
cock&balls Sam drew
when she passed out first at that party.

Now there's a doughnut of rubber smoke
and exhaust where her hair used to hang,

pale greenlit Lincoln
Tunnel instead of a heartbeat,

sighs and eyelashes have become
clouds running in front of the sun.

Adolescent

Oh hell,
I borrowed
Hannah's orange shirt
but the boys can still see
I have breasts,
there they are,
silver ring on a silver chain
glimmering between them.

We threw walnuts,
cat toys, Skittles,
up Girl Power signs,

laughed at rich kids,
at my parents,

touched your father's gun,

pissed off
the back porch,
the cops,

broke
the sliding door
to shards with my own head

and I was not there
for any of it,
I was trapped
in this orange straightjacket,
hair burning,
I remember the one guy's soft lips.

Crater Face

"The rest are all zits,
this one's a brown recluse bite"
the not-so-
faceless woman said flatly
from behind the counter.
She handed me my cigarettes,
a volcano with a black center
in the middle of her chin.
That was a while back—I remember
nothing else of that beautiful stranger.

Mark

The skeleton on the subway grips
his bag of dirty pennies and nickels; where's
he taking them? To be
washed? Stress-eating
the under-side of his own jaw,
trying to disappear his
lower lip, meanwhile
his eyes bug out worse
than Bette Davis—
where's he going,
moon-cold in his tall hat?
Taking those coins
he got out of grates
to pay Chiron to grant
him safe passage
across the tracks?

Year of the Bird Man

There was always something
a little off about your first lay.

His apathy when you kissed,
his stare
wild squint
into dead space
scanning the yard for worms.
His beak, his strange, small, pointed tongue. His mop,
less Ringo, more blue gray
than that.
His total transformation
into a giant winged thing,
pale eggshell cool.

Letter to a Dead Man

Where do we go from here, Ed?
To a city of fog and high walls
on that island you always rave about
in the middle of the Dead Sea
where shit floats
salty to the top?
This is not a stranger.
This is me you're talking to.

Yesterday I brought your favorite,
paprika deviled eggs
and your yellow safety scissors
to cut up shreds of paper
from glossy magazines.
They wouldn't let you have them.
I don't know how to be tender, Ed. Help me.

In your room, I saw blood
trickle down your palms
in stigmata, holy release.
Your face, scratched
from your makeshift briar crown,
forced a derisive laugh
into a wrecked smile
beneath the long hair you insist looks more godlike.

If they'd let me in after visiting hours
I'd stroke your cheek and heal your cuts
with my spit.
I don't know how to be tender, Ed. Help me.

You stand in your underwear
messianic cackle from the edge of the bed
that you can show them the way.
You've proved nothing.
Now you've waded too far out
into the shit-filled sea.

April: For a Friend Whom I Consider Dead

Mistress, forgive this disobedience, this need sprung
from the aquamarine tear ducts and dry heaves
of my midsummer. I just wanted the company.
Friendship locked our arms and we caroled,
snaredrum staccato, over the hill-towns'
deathless valleys (we wished they'd just die),
dreaming and picking nicks
in our own skins. Our only sins
were floating in our own wept
pools, weightless astronauts furnished with Goldschläger,
freight, cargo of sun stares.
It was that carelessness we could not master.

Date Night

6:30 Friday evening
we went skating, surrounded
by a hive of nasal voices.
Attached at the wrists, a two-person carousel,
we went sprawling end over end
like jacks on the ice.
I cut my face on your boot blade, it bled
till the chill froze the hot flow.

Sulking, smoking under the sign
that said NO SMOKING,
I imagined us: you a troll,
me a windup ballerina,
full of movement,
twirling out of the jewelry box,
off the vanity into the floor.
I wouldn't call it "making love,"
exactly.

Stuttering Aubade

There is something I have to tell you, sweet Beth . . .
I have something, I have a someone, someone, you couldn't know because you
don't know like you don't know why I use a word like lascivious to describe you,
an unnecessary word a long word a stam-
-mering lisping word lascivious
don't know why your touch hurts me
hurts me the way I am hurting him because I hurt;
he wants us to go to South America to find mermaids, Prague to find god on the
steps of the Orthodox cathedrals mumbling about being blind, can't look for god
or mermaids or anything if he won't step outside his front door.
He's probably drinking coffee right now waiting for somebody to give him
permission to do what he wants to do or maybe he doesn't want to do it
My God
I have no control over my own night move-
-ments imagining what he'll say tomorrow or today as it's now tomorrow
toss rotate toss spin shift again tell me you know I can't expect you to
tell me you hope I can sleep because you know I can't I can't expect you to
know it

Marry Me

Cups his hands
to a woman's green waist
slumps to his knees
tearing off shorts
to reveal hip and pubic bone.

Overhead, grease fire stains, hums of a naked lightbulb,
moths fluttering. Touch your nose.

Blind   deaf   learning
how it is
to be blind and deaf

(red-orange
of his eyelid
when there's light
in front of it,
when wet beads
drip down his forehead,
when to wipe it off).

A door slams. A wall of glass shatters.
Indifference.   Darkness.   Silence.

He thinks
she is still standing
in the hot room
but she is gone, all
but a chipped fingernail crescent;
smile of smoke-dingy pearls,
bowl of the rising moon.

No Exit

How can I describe
my jealous lust for you?
The best thing to do
is get it through the lips and off the tongue
then sit in shameful silence.
Beauty: angles of a sharp face
softened by choppy blonde
easy smile peach fuzz
grey squint eyes wire biceps
pitch perfect lady makeup.
I must look
strange to you—I dress
backwards and to the left,
hairy legs unplucked eyebrows and all.

There is a photo of us together,
your head hangs lower than mine
and fits in the crook of my arms and we merge,
twin onyx pupils,
lovely little you and broad-shouldered me.
You dance on tiny hot feet burning in silver sandals,
hide in my shoulder and chuckle.
It rings out in notes:
Christ, how you use my eyes
as a mirror to paint your lips,
Christ, your thighs squeezing around my waist,
Christ my big inkstained hands.

A Girl in (Jackson) Library

At the beginning of the century,
she Xeroxes her handouts
on proper hygiene for nutrition class.
She is fair and her pony-bob
bounces precisely en pointe
every time her head moves.
Smiley face-centered daisies
are painted on her toes
in pink green and yellow
(for Easter?).
She is taking up all the space
in front of the machines
and I am tapping my dirty
motorcycle
boot.
Her friend, brunette,
squatty and huge-assed,
flips her bug-eyed sunglasses
up to her forehead,
and stares at me and huffs.
I compare my decade-old
clamshell wireless telephone
to their new ones in pink rubber casings
like stupid helmets.
They're always getting texts.
My mother calls me sometimes.
Up to my face I crumple
a nosebled wad of toilet
paper and blow heavy green snot,
the two girls look so disgusted
at my lack of proper hygiene
that they back away
with their mushroom faces
and I can finally finish
making a copy of my
pompous fucking essay on Dryden.

Evening on Karl Johan Street

Waiting for a woman in the downy evening
makes a man uneasy, especially
because all women
are indistinguishable
from lamp-posts in their Victorian garb.
If you're a man
on a Norwegian street
and you are greeted with a soft smile
from a face that is not yet a corpse,
there's a translucent moment
before she walks on
and is met by the man she was meeting.
You realize she was untightening her lips
at a ghost behind you;
you feel so strange and mawkish,
stared at for split seconds at a time
by people on their way
from pastures of daytime commerce,
corralled into operas and restaurants of night.
There is no loneliness worse
than mistaken recognition
as the slack jawed crowds go around you,
not even looking at you where you're stopped
dead center, on the wrong side of the street.

From the Painting by Edvard Munch

Summer

Person on bubbling pavement outside the deli
sticking her head in cars to ask for change,
black-blocked buildings with Tetris walls smelling
of vegan burgers cooked on gas ranges
and lemongrass organic cleaning solvent.
I ate mealy apples, a caned man shattered
the window. Stoned in public but I felt absolved,
chalky hand prints on the sidewalk. Fractured
reality swilling beer in a kiddie pool
in a poufy bra and sheer panties, squint
out my Dennis Hopper eye at the lifted El
Dorado at the drive-in restaurant,
the woman bouncing her beautiful purple-thonged ass
atop it, being herself, showing us.

Cicada

Who let it in?
It's trapped in the glass bowl
under the bulb in the great room,
fine rattles of fuzz
in the hot night.
—Now louder, catastrophic bullroar,
S.O.S. blinks of brightness—
it shakes itself free, a shock, a dark room,
a whirring golf ball to the face,
the neighbor baby howls,
it's like an air raid.
The insect falls to the hearth, helplessly rolling
in the fine mud of ash and spilled beer
at the chimney base.
Party guests choke bravery into their mouths,
yell and fly for dish towels.
I'm not afraid. I never was.
Tiny sputtering motor
between two fingers,
a pinch ends it.

Shelter from the Storm

Outside the window
view from the roof of the shed
ten feet to dry land; the skies
are filling the potted plants,
they have spattered
the freckled sidewalk
and scattered bits of pine straw.

A crack rips the sky like a rip
in the jagged glass,
crude, echoed
on your flushed forehead.
Break the shards, burn them
and melt them like fat off the bone.

Killing Light

I
Airy strains of peach nectar,
the water from the river
carries ice instead of foam,
melts as it jambs the mud bank, the young
slide into pinkwhite blossoms
which open (the smell, the belly)
as gutted fish. Just as faint violins
echo green pastures of the Lord,
so bells in stone churches bleat.
Newborn things blink and squint
and open their mouths for hot milk.
Everything is open, open.

II
Through a dark cloud of gnats
the sun sets late, you hear
brassy buskers and throw hot quarters
into their hats. Heat and stench of bodies
stuck with sweat in stuffy midnight rooms,
smoke blown out of a bathroom window.
Sleeping outdoors
a mattress on the roof
saves you from suffocation.
You peel grass from your skin
after a too-warm nap.
You peel the skin from soft yams
to avoid getting sick.

III
When things turn orange
and ripen the rotting smell
is intoxicating—and the sounds
they make when thumped!—
hollow plucked buzzes.
Where we are, distant mountains
stretch as high as smoke rings
from dead cottages, dispassionate lips
brush slighter versions of themselves.

There is no bath tub here,
only a rusty cold spigot
that will freeze soon.
How will we bathe our bodies?

IV
All things are dead.
Evergreen trees make a sighing sound
when they sag, their branches
beholden to so many icicles.
"Saint Louis Blues"
again, with feeling—
there is a cup full
of bourbon-melted ice
on the bedside table.
I have one of my fits
and crash my car, Bessie
all the while roars:
I hate to see the evening sun go down.

Vacuum

there is an earthy quiet   just a large hole
filling the eardrums with gravel
punctured by breaths   and beats   pauses
there is this deadness
I fear this deadness
this heavy air
       and I hope that I will never

there being fractions of static and white
particles between sentences

have to strain my ears in eternal calm
though the essence of still allows for unconscious stiffness

in a dark room of extinguished halogens   colors as they are   all blue-
                                                                                   black and gray

prophets sit in their corners   trail carbon dioxide   people go into trances filled
with the Spirit

it's all very stupid

I see no use in trying to prolong
the aching gape of solitude they call enlightenment
or death
                       I do hunger for this quiet
and dread it
every time I sit alone with myself to myself
who cares   I think   I'm not here

Audition

"the darkness sur-
rounds us, what
can we do against
it"
    —Robert Creeley

A letter for me Monday.
No return address.
"I'm sorry for your loss,
John." It told me.
John's not my name.
I felt hairs prickling
around my scalp, nape
of my neck, so I shaved
them off, in the process
slivered away some skin,
because the phone was so loud
when it rang. I dropped it

trying to answer it.
On the other end
a woman's voice, decrepit
nails in plaster walls, said:
"Hey. It's your neighbor Sue.
Don't be alarmed
if you see smoke
over the hill; it's not
the house on fire.
We're burning leaves."
I have no neighbor Sue.
She called me my grandfather's name.

I choked out "wrong number."
Then it was four,
the air thick and early
in my lungs,
I stomped ashes
and up curled stale white rings
looking waifish and chalky

as my likeness
did in the sliding glass
door I was facing.
A rustle in the bush
made me freeze,
my eye trailed near
the place it was
behind me in the glass.

A frail-limbed lump,
its hands and feet
were severed and cauterized,
its head full of teeth
at splintered angles catching gleaming sparks,
grunting. Without turning
from my own glistening
reflection, I lovingly kissed
the nape of its neck
where the scalp had been shaved.

**Fire Woman/
Ice Man**

I once had a vision of somebody in flames
spinning swiftly from the dark woods into a field
grand orange cyclone
lifting her hands higher and higher

and I was glad I was not her, but here
in this silver, this sliver
sticking reflective
in my craw

and without knowing it I punish strangers
who want to know me

Between Two Rivers

the windows are shut
we are naked
there is no other world
but this cigarette dust-
ridden house
I close my eyes
a python is hanging
upside down from the tree
outside and a fluttering
of wings, you trace
from the curve of my breast
to my belly button
I am awake

Cohesion at 3:00

A room of book-lined walls with shelves like mouths,
anthologies for teeth to gape and swarm
their leafy razors over dinner guests,
unfinished poems wadded on the floor,
stale cigarettes, an overfilled trash can,
clothes left to lie where they were taken off,
impatient sounds of scurrying flying squirrels
with big eyes that get through cracks in the roof—
all of these things so clutter up the mind.
To live in such a dusty, stuffy place
is suicide to cohesion. So you walk.

Dead silence meets you when you cross the bridge
into the sparsely populated burg
where you have settled in. Over the edge
of a small bay that forms a lake, the ducks
have ceased to float. There's not even a sound
of rushing water or of jumping fish
who scoop the dragonflies out of midair
with lippy gobs. The hexagon of brick
across the street is where they keep more books.
Its orange light refracts, unnatural—
not even two cars parked suspiciously
to give appearance of a shady drug-deal;
there's no one here. No nosy cops. Walk on
beneath a building sick in its foundations,
go past the sea-rose plants with their odd, red
fruit pods whose tentacles crowd in at dusk.

The moon shines on the water's silty bilge
reflecting off green broken bits of bottle.
So, silent, cold, and ornery, now still
of mind, you squat down at the balmy shore.
It feels as justified as anything
when, like a milk shake, you suck up the bay,
the whole scene, through a thick, striped, purple straw.

1949

Grandmother lived
in a wallpapered chicken-house,
the stove spewing black ash
from leftover hogfeed corncobs in winter.

At nineteen, she married Grandfather
whose job it was to dump hog guts
from slaughter into the river.
Once he dragged especially lumpy entrails
—they had hooves and teeth—
a sow's slit belly toppled
eleven stillborn piglets
the men threw downstream.
The landowners were furious at the loss,

but no one knew what to do;
my aunt was born, red-faced, next summer.

Organ Harvest: Laconia

I died. My body lived. I was a walking tumor,
and then my body understood
how trees must feel
about the warty knots
that seep in through their roots, the saplings
use their decomposing bark
to grow themselves a future. I can grow whole fingers,
keratin nails and all, in my stomach,
but I won't brag about it.
Just get my lymphs and liver
while it's all still good.

Every Photograph of You is a Photograph of When You Were Younger

The sky out here
is a sunless white-grey
with black rings
—those are vultures—
somber nuns vomiting onto their feet
holding their ecclesiastic judgments
between two-pronged, raw, crimson toes.
This is where you got your hennaed hair,
not from red mud but from microscopic
scraps of mica in the sand.
Once the clay's color,
your tresses are now bone-silver
and your face resembles old leather.
Your tracks mark drawings
of what you must have looked like
before the vultures got you,
like those huge sand drawings
in the Southwestern desert—
jackals, tarantulas, and big-breasted women.
They are coming
you say, delirious, pointing
at the vulture circles and wounded earth.
They are coming. They can fly.

The Thing About Shapes in Lookinglasshouse

This orangutan shot
me full of lasers in the mirror this morning
with its red-brown eyes

combed its sparse hair back
and made kissy-mug faces at me like
it knew I had something

inside me that wanted to smash
glass with my fists. It drew lipstick rings
on the wrong part

of its own face
and cackled hysterically clapping its hands
then I turned away

like I got an eyelash
in my eye (wouldn't stop tearing) and I turned back
and my face also returned

and the ape was no longer
in the glass. It wasn't a window anymore
but I'm still waiting.

I Didn't Believe the Stories

Sunday, smoking
outside my grandmother's house
I saw a grasshopper on the brick stoop
being devoured by ants.
Its legs flailed wildly
as the hungry ones a hundredth of its size
bit it to death.

I wanted to end its suffering
but I was barefooted.

"Getting old ain't the end of the world. Dying is."
For John

This house eats things:
ham, bread, Scotch
bottles, whole jars
of paprika, elephant ears,
hog legs, toy cars,
boots and antique brooches, and in the night it freezes
as bodies bumble and crash around mountains
of papers and cubed-glass ice,
wake the neighbors, trash the fountain
with your motorbike, a spoon
clatters into the sink.
This house eats things and it's eating me,
stood in this room like a baby
nuzzling its own fist and my thick
drunk heels tripped back
into a termite hole. I toppled
down a few inches, nearly screamed
at this pit through the center of the Earth as I fell,
not towards or away from anything, dark as death,
Endless Space Forever.

Space Baby

I feel cold, suspended in cold
gel, absence of light, the absent eye, the phantom limb, the tongue that moves
sans musculature. In the grass hut they took me to watch
seventy-eight Marlon Brandos be slaughtered (seventy-eight times!)
until my eyes teared a sticky milk. I'm too full, I filled
up on costly seedy marble
rye. Sucked myself into myself, mean void, blasted-
eardrums void, suspended in nothing, made out of nothing,
nothing,
nothing, nothing.

Space Dogs

Your face in darkness
outlined in silver fireworks
named all the trees in the yard:
Oak
Magnolia
Dogwood
and the birds:
Cardinal
Sparrow
Barn Owl
and the foods we ate:
Sweet Potato
Hawaiian Roll
Green Bean
and the dogs:
Laika
Belka
Strelka
the space dogs that floated
up to the Man in the Moon,
which was also your face
there in the cheery darkness

Pine Inlet

Breathe, boy.
Do not drown. Not here.
Cringe in the wind
that tousles the shallow-root trees.
Your eyes are so wide I can see
to the back of your skull.
You tread water all right.
The Long Leafs surround us—I could drop
this rope, but I won't. It burns
my hands, but I'm pulling
you in.

Hanging Rock Lake

And the girl flew off the cliff into the deep,
And she never was heard tell from ever again.

Oaks in the wind sound like old doors
slamming, that place near my house
(no one saw it for real) just like the movie. False
eyewitness accounts with the same snowy fuzz
as the great bigfoot just out
of the shot at least were pleasant:

Her frame was so small, her bones so starved,
She like caught an updraft, blanketing down.

Bridge Overlooking the Seine

That man lives in *that* house, the one, the one
with the light in the window. Offers a large stone
to the old woman, the old woman hunched
on the bridge and says, "Lick it! Lick it!
Yes, that's how you know it's going to rain.
The air tastes the same, doesn't it?" He laughs.
I can barely see them from here, sun's making
my right eye twitch and head tingle, tremolo
of reeds, of reeds in the ominous, late flutter.
He isn't wrong. That acid aftertaste
of metal. The whole sky is crouching, crouching
over to heave its fecund clouds on us.
I know he is right. He is crazy.

From the Painting by Vincent Van Gogh

Disturbing Portrait of my Father, Sketched by my Grandmother

Think of a man in a dream and you have the same mouth,
same eyes, same nose, and a vacant strange
feeling. You lock others out. It's like
a seizure. Those eyes are dead. Dead.
Trying to listen and not condescend but dead.
You know it. You've felt it. That hollowness. Who is he looking at
just out of frame? Who is he talking to? Do you know?

OH!

The artist forgot to add any light reflecting in the pupils!

Janus

Stop wearing my face for a mask.
Stop wearing my face for a mask.
Sick evil thing living in a deep pit,
I said stop wearing my face for a mask.

Sick evil thing living in a deep pit
on another world like another me
had just the same life, wears my face for a mask

and it screams at the crows in the yard,
puts out two cat's eyes for them,
god-watching marbles, and listens
for rodents in the pipes, but no,

the sick evil thing living in a deep pit
is me, there is one of pure good
at the bottom of some ocean, one sock on,

naked, waiting to cross the Atlantean street.
I have to stop wearing my face for a mask,
peel off this rubber effigy I made
to expose the underneath bile, black

as rust or old menstrual blood
so the good one with one sock
like a stopped watch
can get back moving again.

Parish Priest

For centuries this man's fingers have seeded
goldleafy script of great deeds—like,
how does he keep writing them???

No one has ever seen him, they don't know
anything about the succulent plants he uses to sustain himself,
the tantric binding of genitals,
the species, long-extinct, of beast
that he may have invented,
horned and feathered and
of questionable size.

No they've never seen him nor
his forty-five demon-cat-wives,
the kind who steal your shoes on pagan holidays,
the stone alcove he puts his hay bed on,

the Latin he chants, each measured breath
poking out his soft lips, to the stars,
writing, writing, seventy or
however many chimps on typewriters
churning out his nonsense for eons.

Ars Poetica

Start with words.
Word. Woe. Wood.
Dog. Dogwood. A wooden dog.
Can't stand the sight of it?
Rushing, throw
it out the window in a fit
of splinters and shards
and of shrill yells
splitting the dark.
Cussed. Concussed. That head has an open wound
where a whole person
worth of person leaped out
then slowly died. Really poor job you did
stitching that back up.
The lines aren't even.

Fragments of Buson

When I shut my eyes
The shadow play
spiraled downward,
funnel of rainbow glass
twisting into the abyss, a picture
of Japanese farmers in a field
haunted by a silent music,
like pinpoints on a pianola spool,
a visible notation.
I awoke and my buddy's eye
was next to mine,
deep as a sea shell.
What a perfect moving painting
you are, I told him.

Wedding Poem

beautiful country boy
relieving yourself in a field
let me do that

come lie on my blanket
let me show you
my favorite shapes in the clouds

Domesticity

Onion hands can never be washed
enough; burn our insides
so then husband kisses taste
of onions also.

Revelations

How did we get
to this strange
dark planet
with its yellow heedle-ing
clouds, thundering like
stockinged foot-
falls down the stairs,
the oceans frozen
mid-wave, mid-typhoon,,
stopped,,,

mid-everything.

Everything
is still. So why
are you shaking? There's nothing
to even play
at stoicism about, hold me,,
be quiet,,,

be still.

Wake.

From the Painting by John Valadez

Parish Priest Redux

A man on a thousand squares of light at once,
a brown-haired man whose voice is clear and bright
and young and cross with us is selling us toothpaste,
apple fritters, new tires, bottled drinks,
eyeliner and polygamy.
"*Now is the time!*" he says,
"*The time is now! The time is ripe, the time is a tomato, the time is a ripe tomato, Time the Tomato,*"
the tomato is my heart, he has squeezed
all the juice and the seeds
out of it. The man is
licking the filthiest, the most sacred parts of my heart off the floor like a dog.

America

America is Abraham Lincoln, George Armstrong Custer, and Patsy Cline. America is revision. America is great. America is great, is great, is great. Is a June bug's buzz on a buntinged Mississippi steam boat and pie. America is great. America is great, America is charming, America is quaint coral statuettes of deities like Kali or a dollar sign or amphibian gills from the Black Lagoon or old taste buds falling off your tongue, a rebellious gesture. Great, Great America, the Osirisless Memphis, the Aspic Antilles, the little dots of blood like cherry blooms all over the map of it, little dots like pins, the Paris, Texas Ripper struck again and we connect the dots with a waltz of yarn. America the Just, America the Good King Solomon, America that would cut your baby in half with abacus precision, towering Sinai, towering inferno of Vienna Wieners, in the Atlanta sun, the boiling, needing-to-be-patched Atlanta pavement.

Over the Border

I

i
Draw. Draw a road.
Draw a road. Where's it go? Draw the things
you'd like to see on the road, then
ignore them out
of the monstrous quaking
fear in your gutsack when you pass
them by—don't look!—a robber, a flood, a man
hand held out to you as if
in a dream and he says *here take it take it*
a sweaty wad of twenties and you don't because
there must be something wrong.

ii
The sky is
going to open,
I feel it.

II

i
Here there are things no one has touched, or should.
Small lizards change their skins, the rocks
change that they are rocks. I abhor change,
but I can't stand waiting around for things to happen.

ii
Slowly, slowly
and without much
warning, we find
our own outlooks.

iii
Get
in
the
god
damned
car.

The earth is moving, crusty exoskeletal
giant orphans are resurfacing, we haven't got time
for you to whine about your pangs. Move.

Original Drawings by Ken Kesey

Love Lies Sleeping II

The weird niece on the Munsters
had the ability
to harmonize with herself
so you thought there were
two voices coming out
of her body.
              I heard
two people breathing
in the dark bed, one
from a damp cavern deep
in your chest, one from your dry
whistling nose. I was
afraid at first, then
I understood both sounds
were you, both ebbs and swells

and I had stopped breathing

altogether. Like waking
in the middle of an ocean
and realizing I was not falling,
I was floating.

Awake

The lungs.
The heart.
The stomach.
The heart.
The pain.
The heart.
The hot brain yawns.
The dark tumors,
coiled knots consuming the body like Ouroboros.
The place on the human back where wings would grow,
the glowing skeleton on a black body suit.
The dog's muscles ripple
caged-panther
as she leaps through the air.

100 BPM

For Logie

Don't piss on me for how I grieve,
looking at absences, spaces
where people were, and are not now,
having Alka Seltzer
dissolved into salt-and-pepper
flakes on the TV,
shadowing behind me on a
walk, or breathing on
my neck in the rhythm in which
they breathed, behind my driver's seat.

Every Time I Hear You Cough I Think You're Dying

Past the old
home-stead my mother
put her hand
out the car
window, the air
foggy with pink
dusk. "Right here,
spot's right here.
This altitude, longitude,
latitude is where
I miss Daddy
most." She claims
the air feels
most different there.
Heavy. Cold. Wet.
She says every
missing person has
at least one.
Every living person's
spot for each
missing person varies,
this is called
grief.
         And the
afternoon light falls
over a hanging
strand of your
hair; it blooms
almost-purple-black and silver.

Halo

Pulse of a thousand suns travels
like light down copper wire.
Clouds over nine p.m.,
they gather, they shake
delicately. Men send photos to their wives
from the supermarket
where they've been stationed
for what seems like days.
If I were a sailor I would now take
refuge in the simplicity of childhood,
the enclave of the mind's walls,
the egg that is the inside of the heart.
Everything has the sound of one glass bell in my ear.

Heaven and Earth

Every corridor a hall of mirrors,
                all of mirrors,
                        of mirrors,
      —ors
                corrid—
      —ors
pours
tea/sea
water from a mouth to a lake
                        ache
my pointed stomach, a mask
for someone else's face, aches
is (a) home.
My resting body owns
this couch
        —ed house
of mirrors,

Icarus(Buddha), where have my wing-spans gone,
you've replaced them
and my hair
with air
with darkness,
my listening
expressionless face with light, with
someone else's empty stomach

        ...

Looking at Ink Drawings of Shin Taga

After Man

Midwood in spring all you can hear
is the fluster of birds surprised out of gullies
The Lord's Prayer is the call of a mourning dove.
Gone are the polystyrene floors,
the bus stations and tire treads and intellectual postures,
the hellish foundry threshold Dante must have
crossed to find the center of the Earth.
You are in a place devoid
of human mechanics and fear.
A former paddock contained maybe a horse and pig,
now only rusted earthmovers
covered over with whole,
woody tenants.
Nothing ever happened here,
only creeping lichens, only
a parcel of snails caucusing, laughing at nothing.

Like Frida Kahlo's Burning Bed

When your legs left the ground
where did you go?
Were you on fire? Were you
one of the papery black skeletons against
a dark blue immolated by a flaming moon?
In protest?
In anger?
Or some other reason?
Did
you
smell
the sulfur,
yellow, eggy?
Do you remember someone
now dead
who used to smell
like that? Why do birds
suddenly fill the sky's eye
willy-nilly, no patterns?
Where are they flying and why
can't they work it out? Why

did your legs leave the ground?
Didn't you see
all the tiny wooden
toy soldier-sized
Game of Life village people with piano wire pitchforks
slide themselves off
the edge of that ravine?
Why didn't you try to stop them?
Did you try to stop them?

Al Russell is a human person from North Carolina, United States. Their interests include dairy products, wearing cool hats, and doing housework in secret. They'd prefer you didn't acknowledge their existence.

www.ingramcontent.com/pod-product-compliance
Lightning Source LLC
Chambersburg PA
CBHW030349100526
44592CB00010B/884